THE GOSPEL OF MARK

D0293214

THE
GOSPEL OF MARK

New International Version

HODDER &
STOUGHTON

MARK

John the Baptist prepares the way

1 The beginning of the good news about Jesus the Messiah,*a* the Son of God,*b* *2*as it is written in Isaiah the prophet:

'I will send my messenger ahead of you,
who will prepare your way'*c* –
3 'a voice of one calling in the wilderness,
"Prepare the way for the Lord,
make straight paths for him." '*d*

*4*And so John the Baptist appeared in the wilderness, preaching a baptism of repentance for the forgiveness of sins. *5*The whole Judean countryside and all the people of Jerusalem went out to him. Confessing their sins, they were baptised by him in the River Jordan. *6*John wore clothing made of camel's hair, with a leather belt round his waist, and he ate locusts and wild honey. *7*And this was his message: 'After me comes the one more powerful than I, the straps of whose sandals I

---

a 1 Or *Jesus Christ*. *Messiah* (Hebrew) and *Christ* (Greek) both mean *Anointed One*.
b 1 Some manuscripts do not have *the Son of God*.
c 2 Mal. 3:1
d 3 Isaiah 40:3

am not worthy to stoop down and untie. ⁸I baptise you with*e*
water, but he will baptise you with*e* the Holy Spirit.'

The baptism and testing of Jesus

⁹At that time Jesus came from Nazareth in Galilee and was
baptised by John in the Jordan. ¹⁰Just as Jesus was coming up
out of the water, he saw heaven being torn open and the Spirit
descending on him like a dove. ¹¹And a voice came from heav-
en: 'You are my Son, whom I love; with you I am well pleased.'

¹²At once the Spirit sent him out into the wilderness, ¹³and
he was in the wilderness for forty days, being tempted*f* by
Satan. He was with the wild animals, and angels attended him.

Jesus announces the good news

¹⁴After John was put in prison, Jesus went into Galilee, pro-
claiming the good news of God. ¹⁵'The time has come,' he
said. 'The kingdom of God has come near. Repent and believe
the good news!'

Jesus calls his first disciples

¹⁶As Jesus walked beside the Sea of Galilee, he saw Simon
and his brother Andrew casting a net into the lake, for they
were fishermen. ¹⁷'Come, follow me,' Jesus said, 'and I will

---

e 8 Or *in*
f 13 The Greek for *tempted* can also mean *tested*.

send you out to fish for people.' ¹⁸At once they left their nets and followed him.

¹⁹When he had gone a little farther, he saw James son of Zebedee and his brother John in a boat, preparing their nets. ²⁰Without delay he called them, and they left their father Zebedee in the boat with the hired men and followed him.

Jesus drives out an impure spirit

²¹They went to Capernaum, and when the Sabbath came, Jesus went into the synagogue and began to teach. ²²The people were amazed at his teaching, because he taught them as one who had authority, not as the teachers of the law. ²³Just then a man in their synagogue who was possessed by an impure spirit cried out, ²⁴'What do you want with us, Jesus of Nazareth? Have you come to destroy us? I know who you are – the Holy One of God!'

²⁵'Be quiet!' said Jesus sternly. 'Come out of him!' ²⁶The impure spirit shook the man violently and came out of him with a shriek.

²⁷The people were all so amazed that they asked each other, 'What is this? A new teaching – and with authority! He even gives orders to impure spirits and they obey him.' ²⁸News about him spread quickly over the whole region of Galilee.

Jesus heals many

²⁹As soon as they left the synagogue, they went with James and John to the home of Simon and Andrew. ³⁰Simon's mother-in-law was in bed with a fever, and they immediately

told Jesus about her. ³¹ So he went to her, took her hand and helped her up. The fever left her and she began to wait on them.

³² That evening after sunset the people brought to Jesus all who were ill and demon-possessed. ³³ The whole town gathered at the door, ³⁴ and Jesus healed many who had various diseases. He also drove out many demons, but he would not let the demons speak because they knew who he was.

Jesus prays in a solitary place

³⁵ Very early in the morning, while it was still dark, Jesus got up, left the house and went off to a solitary place, where he prayed. ³⁶ Simon and his companions went to look for him, ³⁷ and when they found him, they exclaimed: 'Everyone is looking for you!'

³⁸ Jesus replied, 'Let us go somewhere else – to the nearby villages – so that I can preach there also. That is why I have come.' ³⁹ So he travelled throughout Galilee, preaching in their synagogues and driving out demons.

Jesus heals a man with leprosy

⁴⁰ A man with leprosy*g* came to him and begged him on his knees, 'If you are willing, you can make me clean.'

⁴¹ Jesus was indignant.*h* He reached out his hand and

---

g 40 The Greek word traditionally translated *leprosy* was used for various diseases affecting the skin.
h 41 Many manuscripts *Jesus was filled with compassion*

touched the man. 'I am willing,' he said. 'Be clean!' ⁴²Immediately the leprosy left him and he was cleansed.

⁴³Jesus sent him away at once with a strong warning: ⁴⁴'See that you don't tell this to anyone. But go, show yourself to the priest and offer the sacrifices that Moses commanded for your cleansing, as a testimony to them.' ⁴⁵Instead he went out and began to talk freely, spreading the news. As a result, Jesus could no longer enter a town openly but stayed outside in lonely places. Yet the people still came to him from everywhere.

Jesus forgives and heals a paralysed man

2 A few days later, when Jesus again entered Capernaum, the people heard that he had come home. ²They gathered in such large numbers that there was no room left, not even outside the door, and he preached the word to them. ³Some men came, bringing to him a paralysed man, carried by four of them. ⁴Since they could not get him to Jesus because of the crowd, they made an opening in the roof above Jesus by digging through it and then lowered the mat the man was lying on. ⁵When Jesus saw their faith, he said to the paralysed man, 'Son, your sins are forgiven.'

⁶Now some teachers of the law were sitting there, thinking to themselves, ⁷'Why does this fellow talk like that? He's blaspheming! Who can forgive sins but God alone?'

⁸Immediately Jesus knew in his spirit that this was what they were thinking in their hearts, and he said to them, 'Why are you thinking these things? ⁹Which is easier: to say to this paralysed man, "Your sins are forgiven," or to say, "Get up,

take your mat and walk"? ¹⁰But I want you to know that the Son of Man has authority on earth to forgive sins.' So he said to the man, ¹¹'I tell you, get up, take your mat and go home.' ¹²He got up, took his mat and walked out in full view of them all. This amazed everyone and they praised God, saying, 'We have never seen anything like this!'

Jesus calls Levi and eats with sinners

¹³Once again Jesus went out beside the lake. A large crowd came to him, and he began to teach them. ¹⁴As he walked along, he saw Levi son of Alphaeus sitting at the tax collector's booth. 'Follow me,' Jesus told him, and Levi got up and followed him.

¹⁵While Jesus was having dinner at Levi's house, many tax collectors and sinners were eating with him and his disciples, for there were many who followed him. ¹⁶When the teachers of the law who were Pharisees saw him eating with the sinners and tax collectors, they asked his disciples: 'Why does he eat with tax collectors and sinners?'

¹⁷On hearing this, Jesus said to them, 'It is not the healthy who need a doctor, but those who are ill. I have not come to call the righteous, but sinners.'

Jesus questioned about fasting

¹⁸Now John's disciples and the Pharisees were fasting. Some people came and asked Jesus, 'How is it that John's disciples and the disciples of the Pharisees are fasting, but yours are not?'

¹⁹ Jesus answered, 'How can the guests of the bridegroom fast while he is with them? They cannot, so long as they have him with them. ²⁰ But the time will come when the bridegroom will be taken from them, and on that day they will fast.

²¹ 'No one sews a patch of unshrunk cloth on an old garment. Otherwise, the new piece will pull away from the old, making the tear worse. ²² And no one pours new wine into old wineskins. Otherwise, the wine will burst the skins, and both the wine and the wineskins will be ruined. No, they pour new wine into new wineskins.'

Jesus is Lord of the Sabbath

²³ One Sabbath Jesus was going through the cornfields, and as his disciples walked along, they began to pick some ears of corn. ²⁴ The Pharisees said to him, 'Look, why are they doing what is unlawful on the Sabbath?'

²⁵ He answered, 'Have you never read what David did when he and his companions were hungry and in need? ²⁶ In the days of Abiathar the high priest, he entered the house of God and ate the consecrated bread, which is lawful only for priests to eat. And he also gave some to his companions.'

²⁷ Then he said to them, 'The Sabbath was made for man, not man for the Sabbath. ²⁸ So the Son of Man is Lord even of the Sabbath.'

Jesus heals on the Sabbath

3 Another time Jesus went into the synagogue, and a man with a shrivelled hand was there. ² Some of them were looking for a reason to accuse Jesus, so they watched him closely to see if he would heal him on the Sabbath. ³Jesus said to the man with the shrivelled hand, 'Stand up in front of everyone.'

⁴Then Jesus asked them, 'Which is lawful on the Sabbath: to do good or to do evil, to save life or to kill?' But they remained silent.

⁵He looked around at them in anger and, deeply distressed at their stubborn hearts, said to the man, 'Stretch out your hand.' He stretched it out, and his hand was completely restored. ⁶Then the Pharisees went out and began to plot with the Herodians how they might kill Jesus.

Crowds follow Jesus

⁷Jesus withdrew with his disciples to the lake, and a large crowd from Galilee followed. ⁸When they heard all he was doing, many people came to him from Judea, Jerusalem, Idumea, and the regions across the Jordan and around Tyre and Sidon. ⁹Because of the crowd he told his disciples to have a small boat ready for him, to keep the people from crowding him. ¹⁰For he had healed many, so that those with diseases were pushing forward to touch him. ¹¹Whenever the impure spirits saw him, they fell down before him and cried out, 'You are the Son of God.' ¹²But he gave them strict orders not to tell others about him.

Jesus appoints the Twelve

13 Jesus went up on a mountainside and called to him those he wanted, and they came to him. **14** He appointed twelve*a* that they might be with him and that he might send them out to preach **15** and to have authority to drive out demons. **16** These are the twelve he appointed: Simon (to whom he gave the name Peter); **17** James son of Zebedee and his brother John (to them he gave the name Boanerges, which means 'sons of thunder'), **18** Andrew, Philip, Bartholomew, Matthew, Thomas, James son of Alphaeus, Thaddaeus, Simon the Zealot **19** and Judas Iscariot, who betrayed him.

Jesus accused by his family and by teachers of the law

20 Then Jesus entered a house, and again a crowd gathered, so that he and his disciples were not even able to eat. **21** When his family*b* heard about this, they went to take charge of him, for they said, 'He is out of his mind.'

22 And the teachers of the law who came down from Jerusalem said, 'He is possessed by Beelzebul! By the prince of demons he is driving out demons.'

23 So Jesus called them over to him and began to speak to them in parables: 'How can Satan drive out Satan? **24** If a kingdom is divided against itself, that kingdom cannot stand. **25** If a house is divided against itself, that house cannot stand. **26** And if Satan opposes himself and is divided, he cannot stand; his end has come. **27** In fact, no one can enter a strong man's

---

a 14 Some manuscripts *twelve – designating them apostles –*
b 21 Or *his associates*

house without first tying him up. Then he can plunder the strong man's house. 28 Truly I tell you, people can be forgiven all their sins and every slander they utter, 29 but whoever blasphemes against the Holy Spirit will never be forgiven; they are guilty of an eternal sin.'

30 He said this because they were saying, 'He has an impure spirit.'

31 Then Jesus' mother and brothers arrived. Standing outside, they sent someone in to call him. 32 A crowd was sitting round him, and they told him, 'Your mother and brothers are outside looking for you.'

33 'Who are my mother and my brothers?' he asked.

34 Then he looked at those seated in a circle round him and said, 'Here are my mother and my brothers! 35 Whoever does God's will is my brother and sister and mother.'

The parable of the sower

4 Again Jesus began to teach by the lake. The crowd that gathered round him was so large that he got into a boat and sat in it out on the lake, while all the people were along the shore at the water's edge. 2 He taught them many things by parables, and in his teaching said: 3 'Listen! A farmer went out to sow his seed. 4 As he was scattering the seed, some fell along the path, and the birds came and ate it up. 5 Some fell on rocky places, where it did not have much soil. It sprang up quickly, because the soil was shallow. 6 But when the sun came up, the plants were scorched, and they withered because they had no root. 7 Other seed fell among thorns, which grew up and choked the plants, so that they did not bear grain. 8 Still

other seed fell on good soil. It came up, grew and produced a crop, some multiplying thirty, some sixty, some a hundred times.'

⁹Then Jesus said, 'Whoever has ears to hear, let them hear.'

¹⁰When he was alone, the Twelve and the others around him asked him about the parables. ¹¹He told them, 'The secret of the kingdom of God has been given to you. But to those on the outside everything is said in parables ¹²so that,

'"they may be ever seeing but never perceiving,
    and ever hearing but never understanding;
otherwise they might turn and be forgiven!"ᵃ'

¹³Then Jesus said to them, 'Don't you understand this parable? How then will you understand any parable? ¹⁴The farmer sows the word. ¹⁵Some people are like seed along the path, where the word is sown. As soon as they hear it, Satan comes and takes away the word that was sown in them. ¹⁶Others, like seed sown on rocky places, hear the word and at once receive it with joy. ¹⁷But since they have no root, they last only a short time. When trouble or persecution comes because of the word, they quickly fall away. ¹⁸Still others, like seed sown among thorns, hear the word; ¹⁹but the worries of this life, the deceitfulness of wealth and the desires for other things come in and choke the word, making it unfruitful. ²⁰Others, like seed sown on good soil, hear the word, accept it, and produce a crop – some thirty, some sixty, some a hundred times what was sown.'

ᵃ 12 Isaiah 6:9,10

A lamp on a stand

21 He said to them, 'Do you bring in a lamp to put it under a bowl or a bed? Instead, don't you put it on its stand? 22 For whatever is hidden is meant to be disclosed, and whatever is concealed is meant to be brought out into the open. 23 If anyone has ears to hear, let them hear.'

24 'Consider carefully what you hear,' he continued. 'With the measure you use, it will be measured to you – and even more. 25 Whoever has will be given more; whoever does not have, even what they have will be taken from them.'

The parable of the growing seed

26 He also said, 'This is what the kingdom of God is like. A man scatters seed on the ground. 27 Night and day, whether he sleeps or gets up, the seed sprouts and grows, though he does not know how. 28 All by itself the soil produces corn – first the stalk, then the ear, then the full grain in the ear. 29 As soon as the corn is ripe, he puts the sickle to it, because the harvest has come.'

The parable of the mustard seed

30 Again he said, 'What shall we say the kingdom of God is like, or what parable shall we use to describe it? 31 It is like a mustard seed, which is the smallest of all seeds on earth. 32 Yet when planted, it grows and becomes the largest of all garden plants, with such big branches that the birds can perch in its shade.'

³³With many similar parables Jesus spoke the word to them, as much as they could understand. ³⁴He did not say anything to them without using a parable. But when he was alone with his own disciples, he explained everything.

Jesus calms the storm

³⁵That day when evening came, he said to his disciples, 'Let us go over to the other side.' ³⁶Leaving the crowd behind, they took him along, just as he was, in the boat. There were also other boats with him. ³⁷A furious squall came up, and the waves broke over the boat, so that it was nearly swamped. ³⁸Jesus was in the stern, sleeping on a cushion. The disciples woke him and said to him, 'Teacher, don't you care if we drown?'

³⁹He got up, rebuked the wind and said to the waves, 'Quiet! Be still!' Then the wind died down and it was completely calm.

⁴⁰He said to his disciples, 'Why are you so afraid? Do you still have no faith?'

⁴¹They were terrified and asked each other, 'Who is this? Even the wind and the waves obey him!'

Jesus restores a demon-possessed man

5 They went across the lake to the region of the Gerasenes.ᵃ ²When Jesus got out of the boat, a man with an impure spirit came from the tombs to meet him. ³This man lived in the tombs, and no one could bind him anymore, not

---

a 1 Some manuscripts *Gadarenes*; other manuscripts *Gergesenes* even with a chain. ⁴For he had often been chained hand and foot, but he tore the chains apart and broke the irons on his feet. No one was strong enough to subdue him. ⁵Night and day among the tombs and in the hills he would cry out and cut himself with stones.

⁶When he saw Jesus from a distance, he ran and fell on his knees in front of him. ⁷He shouted at the top of his voice, 'What do you want with me, Jesus, Son of the Most High God? In God's name don't torture me!' ⁸For Jesus had said to him, 'Come out of this man, you impure spirit!'

⁹Then Jesus asked him, 'What is your name?'

'My name is Legion,' he replied, 'for we are many.' ¹⁰And he begged Jesus again and again not to send them out of the area.

¹¹A large herd of pigs was feeding on the nearby hillside. ¹²The demons begged Jesus, 'Send us among the pigs; allow us to go into them.' ¹³He gave them permission, and the impure spirits came out and went into the pigs. The herd, about two thousand in number, rushed down the steep bank into the lake and were drowned.

¹⁴Those tending the pigs ran off and reported this in the town and countryside, and the people went out to see what had happened. ¹⁵When they came to Jesus, they saw the man who had been possessed by the legion of demons, sitting there, dressed and in his right mind; and they were afraid. ¹⁶Those who had seen it told the people what had happened to the demon-possessed man – and told about the pigs as well. ¹⁷Then the people began to plead with Jesus to leave their region.

¹⁸As Jesus was getting into the boat, the man who had been demon-possessed begged to go with him. ¹⁹Jesus did not let him, but said, 'Go home to your own people and tell them

how much the Lord has done for you, and how he has had mercy on you.' ²⁰So the man went away and began to tell in the Decapolisᵇ how much Jesus had done for him. And all the people were amazed.

Jesus raises a dead girl and heals a sick woman

²¹When Jesus had again crossed over by boat to the other side of the lake, a large crowd gathered round him while he was by the lake. ²²Then one of the synagogue leaders, named Jairus, came, and when he saw Jesus, he fell at his feet. ²³He pleaded earnestly with him, 'My little daughter is dying. Please come and put your hands on her so that she will be healed and live.' ²⁴So Jesus went with him.

A large crowd followed and pressed round him. ²⁵And a woman was there who had been subject to bleeding for twelve years. ²⁶She had suffered a great deal under the care of many doctors and had spent all she had, yet instead of getting better she grew worse. ²⁷When she heard about Jesus, she came up behind him in the crowd and touched his cloak, ²⁸because she thought, 'If I just touch his clothes, I will be healed.' ²⁹Immediately her bleeding stopped and she felt in her body that she was freed from her suffering.

³⁰At once Jesus realised that power had gone out from him. He turned round in the crowd and asked, 'Who touched my clothes?'

³¹'You see the people crowding against you,' his disciples answered, 'and yet you can ask, "Who touched me?"'

ᵇ 20 That is, the Ten Cities

³²But Jesus kept looking around to see who had done it.
³³Then the woman, knowing what had happened to her, came
and fell at his feet and, trembling with fear, told him the whole
truth. ³⁴He said to her, 'Daughter, your faith has healed you.
Go in peace and be freed from your suffering.'

³⁵While Jesus was still speaking, some people came from
the house of Jairus, the synagogue leader. 'Your daughter is
dead,' they said. 'Why bother the teacher anymore?'

³⁶Overhearing^c what they said, Jesus told him, 'Don't be
afraid; just believe.'

³⁷He did not let anyone follow him except Peter, James
and John the brother of James. ³⁸When they came to the
home of the synagogue leader, Jesus saw a commotion, with
people crying and wailing loudly. ³⁹He went in and said to
them, 'Why all this commotion and wailing? The child is not
dead but asleep.' ⁴⁰But they laughed at him.

After he put them all out, he took the child's father and
mother and the disciples who were with him, and went in
where the child was. ⁴¹He took her by the hand and said to her,
'Talitha koum!' (which means 'Little girl, I say to you, get up!').
⁴²Immediately the girl stood up and began to walk around
(she was twelve years old). At this they were completely astonished. ⁴³He gave strict orders not to let anyone know about
this, and told them to give her something to eat.

---

c 36 Or Ignoring

A prophet without honour

6 Jesus left there and went to his home town, accompanied by his disciples. ²When the Sabbath came, he began to teach in the synagogue, and many who heard him were amazed.

'Where did this man get these things?' they asked. 'What's this wisdom that has been given him? What are these remarkable miracles he is performing? ³Isn't this the carpenter? Isn't this Mary's son and the brother of James, Joseph,ᵃ Judas and Simon? Aren't his sisters here with us?' And they took offence at him.

⁴Jesus said to them, 'A prophet is not without honour except in his own town, among his relatives and in his own home.' ⁵He could not do any miracles there, except lay his hands on a few people who were ill and heal them. ⁶He was amazed at their lack of faith.

Jesus sends out the Twelve

Then Jesus went around teaching from village to village. ⁷Calling the Twelve to him, he began to send them out two by two and gave them authority over impure spirits.

⁸These were his instructions: 'Take nothing for the journey except a staff – no bread, no bag, no money in your belts. ⁹Wear sandals but not an extra shirt. ¹⁰Whenever you enter a house, stay there until you leave that town. ¹¹And if any place

---

a 3 Greek *Joses*, a variant of *Joseph*

will not welcome you or listen to you, leave that place and shake the dust off your feet as a testimony against them.'

¹²They went out and preached that people should repent. ¹³They drove out many demons and anointed with oil many people who were ill and healed them.

John the Baptist beheaded

¹⁴King Herod heard about this, for Jesus' name had become well known. Some were saying,*ᵇ* 'John the Baptist has been raised from the dead, and that is why miraculous powers are at work in him.'

¹⁵Others said, 'He is Elijah.'

And still others claimed, 'He is a prophet, like one of the prophets of long ago.'

¹⁶But when Herod heard this, he said, 'John, whom I beheaded, has been raised from the dead!'

¹⁷For Herod himself had given orders to have John arrested, and he had him bound and put in prison. He did this because of Herodias, his brother Philip's wife, whom he had married. ¹⁸For John had been saying to Herod, 'It is not lawful for you to have your brother's wife.' ¹⁹So Herodias nursed a grudge against John and wanted to kill him. But she was not able to, ²⁰because Herod feared John and protected him, knowing him to be a righteous and holy man. When Herod heard John, he was greatly puzzled*ᶜ*; yet he liked to listen to him.

²¹Finally the opportune time came. On his birthday Herod

---

b 14 Some early manuscripts *He was saying*
c 20 Some early manuscripts *he did many things*

gave a banquet for his high officials and military command-
ers and the leading men of Galilee. ²²When the daughter of*d*
Herodias came in and danced, she pleased Herod and his
dinner guests.

The king said to the girl, 'Ask me for anything you want, and
I'll give it to you.' ²³And he promised her with an oath, 'Whatever you ask I will give you, up to half my kingdom.'

²⁴She went out and said to her mother, 'What shall I ask
for?'

'The head of John the Baptist,' she answered.

²⁵At once the girl hurried in to the king with the request:
'I want you to give me right now the head of John the Baptist
on a dish.'

²⁶The king was greatly distressed, but because of his oaths
and his dinner guests, he did not want to refuse her. ²⁷So he
immediately sent an executioner with orders to bring John's
head. The man went, beheaded John in the prison, ²⁸and
brought back his head on a dish. He presented it to the girl,
and she gave it to her mother. ²⁹On hearing of this, John's
disciples came and took his body and laid it in a tomb.

Jesus feeds the five thousand

³⁰The apostles gathered round Jesus and reported to him
all they had done and taught. ³¹Then, because so many people
were coming and going that they did not even have a chance
to eat, he said to them, 'Come with me by yourselves to a quiet
place and get some rest.'

---

d 22 Some early manuscripts *When his daughter*

³²So they went away by themselves in a boat to a solitary place. ³³But many who saw them leaving recognised them and ran on foot from all the towns and got there ahead of them. ³⁴When Jesus landed and saw a large crowd, he had compassion on them, because they were like sheep without a shepherd. So he began teaching them many things.

³⁵By this time it was late in the day, so his disciples came to him. 'This is a remote place,' they said, 'and it's already very late. ³⁶Send the people away so that they can go to the surrounding countryside and villages and buy themselves something to eat.'

³⁷But he answered, 'You give them something to eat.'

They said to him, 'That would take more than half a year's wages*ᵉ*! Are we to go and spend that much on bread and give it to them to eat?'

³⁸'How many loaves do you have?' he asked. 'Go and see.'

When they found out, they said, 'Five – and two fish.'

³⁹Then Jesus told them to make all the people sit down in groups on the green grass. ⁴⁰So they sat down in groups of hundreds and fifties. ⁴¹Taking the five loaves and the two fish and looking up to heaven, he gave thanks and broke the loaves. Then he gave them to his disciples to distribute to the people. He also divided the two fish among them all. ⁴²They all ate and were satisfied, ⁴³and the disciples picked up twelve basketfuls of broken pieces of bread and fish. ⁴⁴The number of the men who had eaten was five thousand.

---

e 37   Greek *take two hundred denarii*

Jesus walks on the water

45 Immediately Jesus made his disciples get into the boat and go on ahead of him to Bethsaida, while he dismissed the crowd. 46 After leaving them, he went up on a mountainside to pray.

47 Later that night, the boat was in the middle of the lake, and he was alone on land. 48 He saw the disciples straining at the oars, because the wind was against them. Shortly before dawn he went out to them, walking on the lake. He was about to pass by them, 49 but when they saw him walking on the lake, they thought he was a ghost. They cried out, 50 because they all saw him and were terrified.

Immediately he spoke to them and said, 'Take courage! It is I. Don't be afraid.' 51 Then he climbed into the boat with them, and the wind died down. They were completely amazed, 52 for they had not understood about the loaves; their hearts were hardened.

53 When they had crossed over, they landed at Gennesaret and anchored there. 54 As soon as they got out of the boat, people recognised Jesus. 55 They ran throughout that whole region and carried those who were ill on mats to wherever they heard he was. 56 And wherever he went – into villages, towns or countryside – they placed those who were ill in the market-places. They begged him to let them touch even the edge of his cloak, and all who touched it were healed.

That which defiles

7 The Pharisees and some of the teachers of the law who had come from Jerusalem gathered round Jesus ²and saw some of his disciples eating food with hands that were defiled, that is, unwashed. ³(The Pharisees and all the Jews do not eat unless they give their hands a ceremonial washing, holding to the tradition of the elders. ⁴When they come from the market-place they do not eat unless they wash. And they observe many other traditions, such as the washing of cups, pitchers and kettles.ᵃ)

⁵So the Pharisees and teachers of the law asked Jesus, 'Why don't your disciples live according to the tradition of the elders instead of eating their food with defiled hands?'

⁶He replied, 'Isaiah was right when he prophesied about you hypocrites; as it is written:

' "These people honour me with their lips,
　　but their hearts are far from me.
⁷They worship me in vain;
　　their teachings are merely human rules."ᵇ

⁸You have let go of the commands of God and are holding on to human traditions.'

⁹And he continued, 'You have a fine way of setting aside the commands of God in order to observeᶜ your own traditions! ¹⁰For Moses said, "Honour your father and mother,"ᵈ

---

a 4　Some early manuscripts *pitchers, kettles and dining couches*
b 6,7　Isaiah 29:13
c 9　Some manuscripts *set up*
d 10　Exodus 20:12; Deut. 5:16

and, "Anyone who curses their father or mother is to be put to death."ᵉ ¹¹ But you say that if anyone declares that what might have been used to help their father or mother is Corban (that is, devoted to God) – ¹²then you no longer let them do anything for their father or mother. ¹³ Thus you nullify the word of God by your tradition that you have handed down. And you do many things like that.'

¹⁴ Again Jesus called the crowd to him and said, 'Listen to me, everyone, and understand this. ¹⁵ Nothing outside a person can defile them by going into them. Rather, it is what comes out of a person that defiles them.' [16]ᶠ

¹⁷ After he had left the crowd and entered the house, his disciples asked him about this parable. ¹⁸ 'Are you so dull?' he asked. 'Don't you see that nothing that enters a person from the outside can defile them? ¹⁹ For it doesn't go into their heart but into their stomach, and then out of the body.' (In saying this, Jesus declared all foods clean.)

²⁰ He went on: 'What comes out of a person is what defiles them. ²¹ For it is from within, out of a person's heart, that evil thoughts come – sexual immorality, theft, murder, ²²adultery, greed, malice, deceit, lewdness, envy, slander, arrogance and folly. ²³ All these evils come from inside and defile a person.'

Jesus honours a Syro-Phoenician woman's faith

²⁴ Jesus left that place and went to the vicinity of Tyre.ᵍ He entered a house and did not want anyone to know it; yet

---

ᵉ 10 Exodus 21:17; Lev. 20:9
ᶠ 16 Some manuscripts include here the words of 4:23.
ᵍ 24 Many early manuscripts *Tyre and Sidon*

he could not keep his presence secret. 25 In fact, as soon as she heard about him, a woman whose little daughter was possessed by an impure spirit came and fell at his feet. 26 The woman was a Greek, born in Syrian Phoenicia. She begged Jesus to drive the demon out of her daughter.

27 'First let the children eat all they want,' he told her, 'for it is not right to take the children's bread and toss it to the dogs.'

28 'Lord,' she replied, 'even the dogs under the table eat the children's crumbs.'

29 Then he told her, 'For such a reply, you may go; the demon has left your daughter.'

30 She went home and found her child lying on the bed, and the demon gone.

Jesus heals a deaf and mute man

31 Then Jesus left the vicinity of Tyre and went through Sidon, down to the Sea of Galilee and into the region of the Decapolis. *h* 32 There some people brought to him a man who was deaf and could hardly talk, and they begged Jesus to place his hand on him.

33 After he took him aside, away from the crowd, Jesus put his fingers into the man's ears. Then he spat and touched the man's tongue. 34 He looked up to heaven and with a deep sigh said to him, '*Ephphatha!*' (which means 'Be opened!'). 35 At this, the man's ears were opened, his tongue was loosed and he began to speak plainly.

---

h 31 That is, the Ten Cities

³⁶ Jesus commanded them not to tell anyone. But the more he did so, the more they kept talking about it. ³⁷ People were overwhelmed with amazement. 'He has done everything well,' they said. 'He even makes the deaf hear and the mute speak.'

Jesus feeds the four thousand

8 During those days another large crowd gathered. Since they had nothing to eat, Jesus called his disciples to him and said, ² 'I have compassion for these people; they have already been with me three days and have nothing to eat. ³ If I send them home hungry, they will collapse on the way, because some of them have come a long distance.'

⁴ His disciples answered, 'But where in this remote place can anyone get enough bread to feed them?'

⁵ 'How many loaves do you have?' Jesus asked.

'Seven,' they replied.

⁶ He told the crowd to sit down on the ground. When he had taken the seven loaves and given thanks, he broke them and gave them to his disciples to distribute to the people, and they did so. ⁷ They had a few small fish as well; he gave thanks for them also and told the disciples to distribute them. ⁸ The people ate and were satisfied. Afterwards the disciples picked up seven basketfuls of broken pieces that were left over. ⁹ About four thousand were present. After he had sent them away, ¹⁰ he got into the boat with his disciples and went to the region of Dalmanutha.

¹¹ The Pharisees came and began to question Jesus. To test him, they asked him for a sign from heaven. ¹² He sighed

deeply and said, 'Why does this generation ask for a sign? Truly I tell you, no sign will be given to it.' ¹³Then he left them, got back into the boat and crossed to the other side.

The yeast of the Pharisees and Herod

¹⁴The disciples had forgotten to bring bread, except for one loaf they had with them in the boat. ¹⁵'Be careful,' Jesus warned them. 'Watch out for the yeast of the Pharisees and that of Herod.'

¹⁶They discussed this with one another and said, 'It is because we have no bread.'

¹⁷Aware of their discussion, Jesus asked them: 'Why are you talking about having no bread? Do you still not see or understand? Are your hearts hardened? ¹⁸Do you have eyes but fail to see, and ears but fail to hear? And don't you remember? ¹⁹When I broke the five loaves for the five thousand, how many basketfuls of pieces did you pick up?'

'Twelve,' they replied.

²⁰'And when I broke the seven loaves for the four thousand, how many basketfuls of pieces did you pick up?'

They answered, 'Seven.'

²¹He said to them, 'Do you still not understand?'

Jesus heals a blind man at Bethsaida

²²They came to Bethsaida, and some people brought a blind man and begged Jesus to touch him. ²³He took the blind man by the hand and led him outside the village. When he had spat

on the man's eyes and put his hands on him, Jesus asked, 'Do you see anything?'

24 He looked up and said, 'I see people; they look like trees walking around.'

25 Once more Jesus put his hands on the man's eyes. Then his eyes were opened, his sight was restored, and he saw everything clearly. 26 Jesus sent him home, saying, 'Don't even go into*a* the village.'

Peter declares that Jesus is the Messiah

27 Jesus and his disciples went on to the villages around Caesarea Philippi. On the way he asked them, 'Who do people say I am?'

28 They replied, 'Some say John the Baptist; others say Elijah; and still others, one of the prophets.'

29 'But what about you?' he asked. 'Who do you say I am?'

Peter answered, 'You are the Messiah.'

30 Jesus warned them not to tell anyone about him.

Jesus predicts his death

31 He then began to teach them that the Son of Man must suffer many things and be rejected by the elders, the chief priests and the teachers of the law, and that he must be killed and after three days rise again. 32 He spoke plainly about this, and Peter took him aside and began to rebuke him.

33 But when Jesus turned and looked at his disciples, he

_____

a 26 Some manuscripts *go and tell anyone in*

rebuked Peter. 'Get behind me, Satan!' he said. 'You do not have in mind the concerns of God, but merely human concerns.'

The way of the cross

34 Then he called the crowd to him along with his disciples and said: 'Whoever wants to be my disciple must deny themselves and take up their cross and follow me. 35 For whoever wants to save their life*b* will lose it, but whoever loses their life for me and for the gospel will save it. 36 What good is it for someone to gain the whole world, yet forfeit their soul? 37 Or what can anyone give in exchange for their soul? 38 If anyone is ashamed of me and my words in this adulterous and sinful generation, the Son of Man will be ashamed of them when he comes in his Father's glory with the holy angels.'

9 And he said to them, 'Truly I tell you, some who are standing here will not taste death before they see that the kingdom of God has come with power.'

The transfiguration

2 After six days Jesus took Peter, James and John with him and led them up a high mountain, where they were all alone. There he was transfigured before them. 3 His clothes became dazzling white, whiter than anyone in the world could bleach them. 4 And there appeared before them Elijah and Moses, who were talking with Jesus.

5 Peter said to Jesus, 'Rabbi, it is good for us to be here. Let

---

b 35 The Greek word means either *life* or *soul*; also in verses 36 and 37.

us put up three shelters – one for you, one for Moses and one for Elijah.' 6(He did not know what to say, they were so frightened.)

7Then a cloud appeared and covered them, and a voice came from the cloud: 'This is my Son, whom I love. Listen to him!'

8Suddenly, when they looked around, they no longer saw anyone with them except Jesus.

9As they were coming down the mountain, Jesus gave them orders not to tell anyone what they had seen until the Son of Man had risen from the dead. 10They kept the matter to themselves, discussing what 'rising from the dead' meant.

11And they asked him, 'Why do the teachers of the law say that Elijah must come first?'

12Jesus replied, 'To be sure, Elijah does come first, and restores all things. Why then is it written that the Son of Man must suffer much and be rejected? 13But I tell you, Elijah has come, and they have done to him everything they wished, just as it is written about him.'

Jesus heals a boy possessed by an impure spirit

14When they came to the other disciples, they saw a large crowd around them and the teachers of the law arguing with them. 15As soon as all the people saw Jesus, they were overwhelmed with wonder and ran to greet him.

16'What are you arguing with them about?' he asked.

17A man in the crowd answered, 'Teacher, I brought you my son, who is possessed by a spirit that has robbed him of speech. 18Whenever it seizes him, it throws him to the ground.

He foams at the mouth, gnashes his teeth and becomes rigid. I asked your disciples to drive out the spirit, but they could not.'

19 'You unbelieving generation,' Jesus replied, 'how long shall I stay with you? How long shall I put up with you? Bring the boy to me.'

20 So they brought him. When the spirit saw Jesus, it immediately threw the boy into a convulsion. He fell to the ground and rolled around, foaming at the mouth.

21 Jesus asked the boy's father, 'How long has he been like this?'

'From childhood,' he answered. 22 'It has often thrown him into fire or water to kill him. But if you can do anything, take pity on us and help us.'

23 ' "If you can"?' said Jesus. 'Everything is possible for one who believes.'

24 Immediately the boy's father exclaimed, 'I do believe; help me overcome my unbelief!'

25 When Jesus saw that a crowd was running to the scene, he rebuked the impure spirit. 'You deaf and mute spirit,' he said, 'I command you, come out of him and never enter him again.'

26 The spirit shrieked, convulsed him violently and came out. The boy looked so much like a corpse that many said, 'He's dead.' 27 But Jesus took him by the hand and lifted him to his feet, and he stood up.

28 After Jesus had gone indoors, his disciples asked him privately, 'Why couldn't we drive it out?'

29 He replied, 'This kind can come out only by prayer.*'

----

a 29 Some manuscripts *prayer and fasting*

Jesus predicts his death a second time

30They left that place and passed through Galilee. Jesus did not want anyone to know where they were, **31**because he was teaching his disciples. He said to them, 'The Son of Man is going to be delivered into the hands of men. They will kill him, and after three days he will rise.' **32**But they did not understand what he meant and were afraid to ask him about it.

33They came to Capernaum. When he was in the house, he asked them, 'What were you arguing about on the road?' **34**But they kept quiet because on the way they had argued about who was the greatest.

35Sitting down, Jesus called the Twelve and said, 'Anyone who wants to be first must be the very last, and the servant of all.'

36He took a little child whom he placed among them. Taking the child in his arms, he said to them, **37** 'Whoever welcomes one of these little children in my name welcomes me; and whoever welcomes me does not welcome me but the one who sent me.'

Whoever is not against us is for us

38'Teacher,' said John, 'we saw someone driving out demons in your name and we told him to stop, because he was not one of us.'

39'Do not stop him,' Jesus said. 'For no one who does a miracle in my name can in the next moment say anything bad about me, **40**for whoever is not against us is for us. **41**Truly I tell you, anyone who gives you a cup of water in my name because you belong to the Messiah will certainly not lose their reward.

Causing to stumble

42 'If anyone causes one of these little ones – those who believe in me – to stumble, it would be better for them if a large millstone were hung round their neck and they were thrown into the sea. 43 If your hand causes you to stumble, cut it off. It is better for you to enter life maimed than with two hands to go into hell, where the fire never goes out. [44] b 45 And if your foot causes you to stumble, cut it off. It is better for you to enter life crippled than to have two feet and be thrown into hell. [46] b 47 And if your eye causes you to stumble, pluck it out. It is better for you to enter the kingdom of God with one eye than to have two eyes and be thrown into hell, 48 where

' "the worms that eat them do not die,
    and the fire is not quenched." c

49 Everyone will be salted with fire.

50 'Salt is good, but if it loses its saltiness, how can you make it salty again? Have salt among yourselves, and be at peace with each other.'

---

b 44,46 Some manuscripts include here the words of verse 48.
c 48 Isaiah 66:24

Divorce

10 Jesus then left that place and went into the region of Judea and across the Jordan. Again crowds of people came to him, and as was his custom, he taught them.

² Some Pharisees came and tested him by asking, 'Is it lawful for a man to divorce his wife?'

³ 'What did Moses command you?' he replied.

⁴ They said, 'Moses permitted a man to write a certificate of divorce and send her away.'

⁵ 'It was because your hearts were hard that Moses wrote you this law,' Jesus replied. ⁶ 'But at the beginning of creation God "made them male and female".*ᵃ* ⁷ "For this reason a man will leave his father and mother and be united to his wife,*ᵇ* ⁸ and the two will become one flesh."*ᶜ* So they are no longer two, but one flesh. ⁹ Therefore what God has joined together, let no one separate.'

¹⁰ When they were in the house again, the disciples asked Jesus about this. ¹¹ He answered, 'Anyone who divorces his wife and marries another woman commits adultery against her. ¹² And if she divorces her husband and marries another man, she commits adultery.'

The little children and Jesus

¹³ People were bringing little children to Jesus for him to place his hands on them, but the disciples rebuked them.

---

a 6 Gen. 1:27
b 7 Some early manuscripts do not have *and be united to his wife*.
c 8 Gen. 2:24

¹⁴When Jesus saw this, he was indignant. He said to them, 'Let the little children come to me, and do not hinder them, for the kingdom of God belongs to such as these. ¹⁵Truly I tell you, anyone who will not receive the kingdom of God like a little child will never enter it.' ¹⁶And he took the children in his arms, placed his hands on them and blessed them.

The rich and the kingdom of God

¹⁷As Jesus started on his way, a man ran up to him and fell on his knees before him. 'Good teacher,' he asked, 'what must I do to inherit eternal life?'

¹⁸'Why do you call me good?' Jesus answered. 'No one is good – except God alone. ¹⁹You know the commandments: "You shall not murder, you shall not commit adultery, you shall not steal, you shall not give false testimony, you shall not defraud, honour your father and mother."*d*'

²⁰'Teacher,' he declared, 'all these I have kept since I was a boy.'

²¹Jesus looked at him and loved him. 'One thing you lack,' he said. 'Go, sell everything you have and give to the poor, and you will have treasure in heaven. Then come, follow me.'

²²At this the man's face fell. He went away sad, because he had great wealth.

²³Jesus looked round and said to his disciples, 'How hard it is for the rich to enter the kingdom of God!'

²⁴The disciples were amazed at his words. But Jesus said

---

d 19 Exodus 20:12-16; Deut. 5:16-20

again, 'Children, how hard it is[e] to enter the kingdom of God! 25 It is easier for a camel to go through the eye of a needle than for someone who is rich to enter the kingdom of God.'

26 The disciples were even more amazed, and said to each other, 'Who then can be saved?'

27 Jesus looked at them and said, 'With man this is impossible, but not with God; all things are possible with God.'

28 Then Peter spoke up, 'We have left everything to follow you!'

29 'Truly I tell you,' Jesus replied, 'no one who has left home or brothers or sisters or mother or father or children or fields for me and the gospel 30 will fail to receive a hundred times as much in this present age: homes, brothers, sisters, mothers, children and fields – along with persecutions – and in the age to come eternal life. 31 But many who are first will be last, and the last first.'

Jesus predicts his death a third time

32 They were on their way up to Jerusalem, with Jesus leading the way, and the disciples were astonished, while those who followed were afraid. Again he took the Twelve aside and told them what was going to happen to him. 33 'We are going up to Jerusalem,' he said, 'and the Son of Man will be delivered over to the chief priests and the teachers of the law. They will condemn him to death and will hand him over to the Gentiles, 34 who will mock him and spit on him, flog him and kill him. Three days later he will rise.'

---

e 24 Some manuscripts *is for those who trust in riches*

The request of James and John

35 Then James and John, the sons of Zebedee, came to him. 'Teacher,' they said, 'we want you to do for us whatever we ask.'

36 'What do you want me to do for you?' he asked.

37 They replied, 'Let one of us sit at your right and the other at your left in your glory.'

38 'You don't know what you are asking,' Jesus said. 'Can you drink the cup I drink or be baptised with the baptism I am baptised with?'

39 'We can,' they answered.

Jesus said to them, 'You will drink the cup I drink and be baptised with the baptism I am baptised with, 40 but to sit at my right or left is not for me to grant. These places belong to those for whom they have been prepared.'

41 When the ten heard about this, they became indignant with James and John. 42 Jesus called them together and said, 'You know that those who are regarded as rulers of the Gentiles lord it over them, and their high officials exercise authority over them. 43 Not so with you. Instead, whoever wants to become great among you must be your servant, 44 and whoever wants to be first must be slave of all. 45 For even the Son of Man did not come to be served, but to serve, and to give his life as a ransom for many.'

Blind Bartimaeus receives his sight

46 Then they came to Jericho. As Jesus and his disciples, together with a large crowd, were leaving the city, a blind man, Bartimaeus (which means 'son of Timaeus'), was sitting by

the roadside begging. **47** When he heard that it was Jesus of Nazareth, he began to shout, 'Jesus, Son of David, have mercy on me!'

48 Many rebuked him and told him to be quiet, but he shouted all the more, 'Son of David, have mercy on me!'

49 Jesus stopped and said, 'Call him.'

So they called to the blind man, 'Cheer up! On your feet! He's calling you.' **50** Throwing his cloak aside, he jumped to his feet and came to Jesus.

51 'What do you want me to do for you?' Jesus asked him.

The blind man said, 'Rabbi, I want to see.'

52 'Go,' said Jesus, 'your faith has healed you.' Immediately he received his sight and followed Jesus along the road.

Jesus comes to Jerusalem as king

11 As they approached Jerusalem and came to Bethphage and Bethany at the Mount of Olives, Jesus sent two of his disciples, **2** saying to them, 'Go to the village ahead of you, and just as you enter it, you will find a colt tied there, which no one has ever ridden. Untie it and bring it here. **3** If anyone asks you, "Why are you doing this?" say, "The Lord needs it and will send it back here shortly." '

4 They went and found a colt outside in the street, tied at a doorway. As they untied it, **5** some people standing there asked, 'What are you doing, untying that colt?' **6** They answered as Jesus had told them to, and the people let them go. **7** When they brought the colt to Jesus and threw their cloaks over it, he sat on it. **8** Many people spread their cloaks on the road, while others spread branches they had cut in the fields. 9 Those who went ahead and those who followed shouted,

'Hosanna!*a*'

'Blessed is he who comes in the name of the Lord!'*b*

10 'Blessed is the coming kingdom of our father David!'

'Hosanna in the highest heaven!'

11 Jesus entered Jerusalem and went into the temple courts. He looked around at everything, but since it was already late, he went out to Bethany with the Twelve.

Jesus curses a fig-tree and clears the temple courts

12 The next day as they were leaving Bethany, Jesus was hungry. 13 Seeing in the distance a fig-tree in leaf, he went to find out if it had any fruit. When he reached it, he found nothing but leaves, because it was not the season for figs. 14 Then he said to the tree, 'May no one ever eat fruit from you again.' And his disciples heard him say it.

15 On reaching Jerusalem, Jesus entered the temple courts and began driving out those who were buying and selling there. He overturned the tables of the money-changers and the benches of those selling doves, 16 and would not allow anyone to carry merchandise through the temple courts.

a 9 A Hebrew expression meaning 'Save!' which became an exclamation of praise; also in verse 10
b 9 Psalm 118:25,26

¹⁷ And as he taught them, he said, 'Is it not written: "My house will be called a house of prayer for all nations"ᶜ? But you have made it "a den of robbers".ᵈ'

¹⁸ The chief priests and the teachers of the law heard this and began looking for a way to kill him, for they feared him, because the whole crowd was amazed at his teaching.

¹⁹ When evening came, Jesus and his disciplesᵉ went out of the city.

²⁰ In the morning, as they went along, they saw the fig-tree withered from the roots. ²¹ Peter remembered and said to Jesus, 'Rabbi, look! The fig-tree you cursed has withered!'

²² 'Have faith in God,' Jesus answered. ²³ 'Trulyᶠ I tell you, if anyone says to this mountain, "Go, throw yourself into the sea," and does not doubt in their heart but believes that what they say will happen, it will be done for them. ²⁴ Therefore I tell you, whatever you ask for in prayer, believe that you have received it, and it will be yours. ²⁵ And when you stand praying, if you hold anything against anyone, forgive them, so that your Father in heaven may forgive you your sins.' [26]ᵍ

The authority of Jesus questioned

²⁷ They arrived again in Jerusalem, and while Jesus was walking in the temple courts, the chief priests, the teachers of the law and the elders came to him. ²⁸ 'By what authority

---

c 17 Isaiah 56:7
d 17 Jer. 7:11
e 19 Some early manuscripts *came, Jesus*
f 22,23 Some early manuscripts *'If you have faith in God,' Jesus answered,* ²³*'truly*
g 26 Some manuscripts include here words similar to Matt. 6:15.

are you doing these things?' they asked. 'And who gave you authority to do this?'

29 Jesus replied, 'I will ask you one question. Answer me, and I will tell you by what authority I am doing these things. 30 John's baptism – was it from heaven, or of human origin? Tell me!'

31 They discussed it among themselves and said, 'If we say, "From heaven," he will ask, "Then why didn't you believe him?" 32 But if we say, "Of human origin" . . .' (They feared the people, for everyone held that John really was a prophet.)

33 So they answered Jesus, 'We don't know.'

Jesus said, 'Neither will I tell you by what authority I am doing these things.'

The parable of the tenants

12 Jesus then began to speak to them in parables: 'A man planted a vineyard. He put a wall round it, dug a pit for the winepress and built a watchtower. Then he rented the vineyard to some farmers and moved to another place. 2 At harvest time he sent a servant to the tenants to collect from them some of the fruit of the vineyard. 3 But they seized him, beat him and sent him away empty-handed. 4 Then he sent another servant to them; they struck this man on the head and treated him shamefully. 5 He sent still another, and that one they killed. He sent many others; some of them they beat, others they killed.

6 'He had one left to send, a son, whom he loved. He sent him last of all, saying, "They will respect my son."

7 'But the tenants said to one another, "This is the heir.

Come, let's kill him, and the inheritance will be ours." ⁸So they took him and killed him, and threw him out of the vineyard.

⁹'What then will the owner of the vineyard do? He will come and kill those tenants and give the vineyard to others. ¹⁰Haven't you read this passage of Scripture:

' "The stone the builders rejected
    has become the cornerstone;
¹¹ the Lord has done this,
    and it is marvellous in our eyes"ᵃ?'

¹²Then the chief priests, the teachers of the law and the elders looked for a way to arrest him because they knew he had spoken the parable against them. But they were afraid of the crowd; so they left him and went away.

Paying the poll-tax to Caesar

¹³Later they sent some of the Pharisees and Herodians to Jesus to catch him in his words. ¹⁴They came to him and said, 'Teacher, we know that you are a man of integrity. You aren't swayed by others, because you pay no attention to who they are; but you teach the way of God in accordance with the truth. Is it right to pay the poll-taxᵇ to Caesar or not? ¹⁵Should we pay or shouldn't we?'

But Jesus knew their hypocrisy. 'Why are you trying to trap me?' he asked. 'Bring me a denarius and let me look at it.'

---

a 11 Psalm 118:22,23
b 14 A special tax levied on subject peoples, not on Roman citizens

¹⁶ They brought the coin, and he asked them, 'Whose image is this? And whose inscription?'

'Caesar's,' they replied.

¹⁷ Then Jesus said to them, 'Give back to Caesar what is Caesar's and to God what is God's.'

And they were amazed at him.

Marriage at the resurrection

¹⁸ Then the Sadducees, who say there is no resurrection, came to him with a question. ¹⁹ 'Teacher,' they said, 'Moses wrote for us that if a man's brother dies and leaves a wife but no children, the man must marry the widow and raise up offspring for his brother. ²⁰ Now there were seven brothers. The first one married and died without leaving any children. ²¹ The second one married the widow, but he also died, leaving no child. It was the same with the third. ²² In fact, none of the seven left any children. Last of all, the woman died too. ²³ At the resurrection^c whose wife will she be, since the seven were married to her?'

²⁴ Jesus replied, 'Are you not in error because you do not know the Scriptures or the power of God? ²⁵ When the dead rise, they will neither marry nor be given in marriage; they will be like the angels in heaven. ²⁶ Now about the dead rising – have you not read in the Book of Moses, in the account of the burning bush, how God said to him, "I am the God of Abraham, the God of Isaac, and the God of Jacob"^d? ²⁷ He is not the God of the dead, but of the living. You are badly mistaken!'

---

c 23 Some manuscripts *resurrection, when people rise from the dead,*
d 26 Exodus 3:6

The greatest commandment

28 One of the teachers of the law came and heard them debating. Noticing that Jesus had given them a good answer, he asked him, 'Of all the commandments, which is the most important?'

29 'The most important one,' answered Jesus, 'is this: "Hear, O Israel: the Lord our God, the Lord is one.e 30 Love the Lord your God with all your heart and with all your soul and with all your mind and with all your strength."f 31 The second is this: "Love your neighbour as yourself."g There is no command-ment greater than these.'

32 'Well said, teacher,' the man replied. 'You are right in say-ing that God is one and there is no other but him. 33 To love him with all your heart, with all your understanding and with all your strength, and to love your neighbour as yourself is more important than all burnt offerings and sacrifices.'

34 When Jesus saw that he had answered wisely, he said to him, 'You are not far from the kingdom of God.' And from then on no one dared ask him any more questions.

Whose son is the Messiah?

35 While Jesus was teaching in the temple courts, he asked, 'Why do the teachers of the law say that the Messiah is the son of David? 36 David himself, speaking by the Holy Spirit, declared:

---

e 29 Or the Lord our God is one Lord
f 30 Deut. 6:4,5
g 31 Lev. 19:18

' "The Lord said to my Lord:
  'Sit at my right hand
until I put your enemies
    under your feet.' "*h*

37 David himself calls him "Lord". How then can he be his son?'
The large crowd listened to him with delight.

Warning against the teachers of the law

38 As he taught, Jesus said, 'Watch out for the teachers of the
law. They like to walk around in flowing robes and be greeted
with respect in the market-places, 39 and have the most important seats in the synagogues and the places of honour at
banquets. 40 They devour widows' houses and for a show make
lengthy prayers. These men will be punished most severely.'

The widow's offering

41 Jesus sat down opposite the place where the offerings
were put and watched the crowd putting their money into the
temple treasury. Many rich people threw in large amounts.
42 But a poor widow came and put in two very small copper
coins, worth only a few pence.

43 Calling his disciples to him, Jesus said, 'Truly I tell you,
this poor widow has put more into the treasury than all the
others. 44 They all gave out of their wealth; but she, out of her
poverty, put in everything – all she had to live on.'

----

h 36 Psalm 110:1

The destruction of the temple and signs of the end times

13 As Jesus was leaving the temple, one of his disciples said to him, 'Look, Teacher! What massive stones! What magnificent buildings!'

2 'Do you see all these great buildings?' replied Jesus. 'Not one stone here will be left on another; every one will be thrown down.'

3 As Jesus was sitting on the Mount of Olives opposite the temple, Peter, James, John and Andrew asked him privately, 4 'Tell us, when will these things happen? And what will be the sign that they are all about to be fulfilled?'

5 Jesus said to them: 'Watch out that no one deceives you. 6 Many will come in my name, claiming, "I am he," and will deceive many. 7 When you hear of wars and rumours of wars, do not be alarmed. Such things must happen, but the end is still to come. 8 Nation will rise against nation, and kingdom against kingdom. There will be earthquakes in various places, and famines. These are the beginning of birth-pains.

9 'You must be on your guard. You will be handed over to the local councils and flogged in the synagogues. On account of me you will stand before governors and kings as witnesses to them. 10 And the gospel must first be preached to all nations. 11 Whenever you are arrested and brought to trial, do not worry beforehand about what to say. Just say whatever is given you at the time, for it is not you speaking, but the Holy Spirit.

12 'Brother will betray brother to death, and a father his child. Children will rebel against their parents and have them put to death. 13 Everyone will hate you because of me, but the one who stands firm to the end will be saved.

¹⁴ 'When you see "the abomination that causes desolation"ᵃ standing where itᵇ does not belong – let the reader understand – then let those who are in Judea flee to the mountains. ¹⁵ Let no one on the housetop go down or enter the house to take anything out. ¹⁶ Let no one in the field go back to get their cloak. ¹⁷ How dreadful it will be in those days for pregnant women and nursing mothers! ¹⁸ Pray that this will not take place in winter, ¹⁹ because those will be days of distress unequalled from the beginning, when God created the world, until now – and never to be equalled again.

²⁰ 'If the Lord had not cut short those days, no one would survive. But for the sake of the elect, whom he has chosen, he has shortened them. ²¹ At that time if anyone says to you, "Look, here is the Messiah!" or, "Look, there he is!" do not believe it. ²² For false messiahs and false prophets will appear and perform signs and wonders to deceive, if possible, even the elect. ²³ So be on your guard; I have told you everything in advance.

²⁴ 'But in those days, following that distress,

' "the sun will be darkened,
     and the moon will not give its light;
²⁵ the stars will fall from the sky,
     and the heavenly bodies will be shaken."ᶜ

²⁶ 'At that time people will see the Son of Man coming in clouds with great power and glory. ²⁷ And he will send his

---

a 14 Daniel 9:27; 11:31; 12:11
b 14 Or *he*
c 25 Isaiah 13:10; 34:4

angels and gather his elect from the four winds, from the ends of the earth to the ends of the heavens.

28 'Now learn this lesson from the fig-tree: as soon as its twigs get tender and its leaves come out, you know that summer is near. 29 Even so, when you see these things happening, you know that it*d* is near, right at the door. 30 Truly I tell you, this generation will certainly not pass away until all these things have happened. 31 Heaven and earth will pass away, but my words will never pass away.

The day and hour unknown

32 'But about that day or hour no one knows, not even the angels in heaven, nor the Son, but only the Father. 33 Be on guard! Be alert*e*! You do not know when that time will come. 34 It's like a man going away: he leaves his house and puts his servants in charge, each with their assigned task, and tells the one at the door to keep watch.

35 'Therefore keep watch because you do not know when the owner of the house will come back – whether in the evening, or at midnight, or when the cock crows, or at dawn. 36 If he comes suddenly, do not let him find you sleeping. 37 What I say to you, I say to everyone: "Watch!" '

---

d 29 Or *he*
e 33 Some manuscripts *alert and pray*

Jesus anointed at Bethany

14 Now the Passover and the Festival of Unleavened Bread were only two days away, and the chief priests and the teachers of the law were scheming to arrest Jesus secretly and kill him. ² 'But not during the festival,' they said, 'or the people may riot.'

³ While he was in Bethany, reclining at the table in the home of Simon the Leper, a woman came with an alabaster jar of very expensive perfume, made of pure nard. She broke the jar and poured the perfume on his head.

⁴ Some of those present were saying indignantly to one another, 'Why this waste of perfume? ⁵ It could have been sold for more than a year's wages*ᵃ* and the money given to the poor.' And they rebuked her harshly.

⁶ 'Leave her alone,' said Jesus. 'Why are you bothering her? She has done a beautiful thing to me. ⁷ The poor you will always have with you,*ᵇ* and you can help them any time you want. But you will not always have me. ⁸ She did what she could. She poured perfume on my body beforehand to prepare for my burial. ⁹ Truly I tell you, wherever the gospel is preached throughout the world, what she has done will also be told, in memory of her.'

¹⁰ Then Judas Iscariot, one of the Twelve, went to the chief priests to betray Jesus to them. ¹¹ They were delighted to hear this and promised to give him money. So he watched for an opportunity to hand him over.

---

a 5 Greek *than three hundred denarii*
b 7 See Deut. 15:11.

The Last Supper

¹²On the first day of the Festival of Unleavened Bread, when it was customary to sacrifice the Passover lamb, Jesus' disciples asked him, 'Where do you want us to go and make preparations for you to eat the Passover?'

¹³So he sent two of his disciples, telling them, 'Go into the city, and a man carrying a jar of water will meet you. Follow him. ¹⁴Say to the owner of the house he enters, "The Teacher asks: where is my guest room, where I may eat the Passover with my disciples?" ¹⁵He will show you a large room upstairs, furnished and ready. Make preparations for us there.'

¹⁶The disciples left, went into the city and found things just as Jesus had told them. So they prepared the Passover.

¹⁷When evening came, Jesus arrived with the Twelve. ¹⁸While they were reclining at the table eating, he said, 'Truly I tell you, one of you will betray me – one who is eating with me.'

¹⁹They were saddened, and one by one they said to him, 'Surely you don't mean me?'

²⁰'It is one of the Twelve,' he replied, 'one who dips bread into the bowl with me. ²¹The Son of Man will go just as it is written about him. But woe to that man who betrays the Son of Man! It would be better for him if he had not been born.'

²²While they were eating, Jesus took bread, and when he had given thanks, he broke it and gave it to his disciples, saying, 'Take it; this is my body.'

²³Then he took a cup, and when he had given thanks, he gave it to them, and they all drank from it.

24 'This is my blood of the^c covenant, which is poured out for many,' he said to them. 25 'Truly I tell you, I will not drink again from the fruit of the vine until that day when I drink it new in the kingdom of God.'

26 When they had sung a hymn, they went out to the Mount of Olives.

Jesus predicts Peter's denial

27 'You will all fall away,' Jesus told them, 'for it is written:

' "I will strike the shepherd,
    and the sheep will be scattered."^d

28 But after I have risen, I will go ahead of you into Galilee.'

29 Peter declared, 'Even if all fall away, I will not.'

30 'Truly I tell you,' Jesus answered, 'today – yes, tonight – before the cock crows twice^e you yourself will disown me three times.'

31 But Peter insisted emphatically, 'Even if I have to die with you, I will never disown you.' And all the others said the same.

Gethsemane

32 They went to a place called Gethsemane, and Jesus said to his disciples, 'Sit here while I pray.' 33 He took Peter, James and John along with him, and he began to be deeply distressed and

---

c 24 Some manuscripts *the new*
d 27 Zech. 13:7
e 30 Some early manuscripts do not have *twice*.

troubled. **34** 'My soul is overwhelmed with sorrow to the point of death,' he said to them. 'Stay here and keep watch.'

35 Going a little farther, he fell to the ground and prayed that if possible the hour might pass from him. **36** *'Abba,f* Father,' he said, 'everything is possible for you. Take this cup from me. Yet not what I will, but what you will.'

37 Then he returned to his disciples and found them sleeping. 'Simon,' he said to Peter, 'are you asleep? Couldn't you keep watch for one hour? **38** Watch and pray so that you will not fall into temptation. The spirit is willing, but the flesh is weak.'

39 Once more he went away and prayed the same thing. **40** When he came back, he again found them sleeping, because their eyes were heavy. They did not know what to say to him.

41 Returning the third time, he said to them, 'Are you still sleeping and resting? Enough! The hour has come. Look, the Son of Man is delivered into the hands of sinners. **42** Rise! Let us go! Here comes my betrayer!'

Jesus arrested

43 Just as he was speaking, Judas, one of the Twelve, appeared. With him was a crowd armed with swords and clubs, sent from the chief priests, the teachers of the law, and the elders.

44 Now the betrayer had arranged a signal with them: 'The one I kiss is the man; arrest him and lead him away under guard.' **45** Going at once to Jesus, Judas said, 'Rabbi!' and

---

f36 Aramaic for *father*

kissed him. ⁴⁶The men seized Jesus and arrested him. ⁴⁷Then one of those standing near drew his sword and struck the servant of the high priest, cutting off his ear.

⁴⁸'Am I leading a rebellion,' said Jesus, 'that you have come out with swords and clubs to capture me? ⁴⁹Every day I was with you, teaching in the temple courts, and you did not arrest me. But the Scriptures must be fulfilled.' ⁵⁰Then everyone deserted him and fled.

⁵¹A young man, wearing nothing but a linen garment, was following Jesus. When they seized him, ⁵²he fled naked, leaving his garment behind.

Jesus before the Sanhedrin

⁵³They took Jesus to the high priest, and all the chief priests, the elders and the teachers of the law came together. ⁵⁴Peter followed him at a distance, right into the courtyard of the high priest. There he sat with the guards and warmed himself at the fire.

⁵⁵The chief priests and the whole Sanhedrin were looking for evidence against Jesus so that they could put him to death, but they did not find any. ⁵⁶Many testified falsely against him, but their statements did not agree.

⁵⁷Then some stood up and gave this false testimony against him: ⁵⁸'We heard him say, "I will destroy this temple made with human hands and in three days will build another, not made with hands." ' ⁵⁹Yet even then their testimony did not agree.

⁶⁰Then the high priest stood up before them and asked Jesus, 'Are you not going to answer? What is this testimony

that these men are bringing against you?' **61** But Jesus remained silent and gave no answer.

Again the high priest asked him, 'Are you the Messiah, the Son of the Blessed One?'

62 'I am,' said Jesus. 'And you will see the Son of Man sitting at the right hand of the Mighty One and coming on the clouds of heaven.'

63 The high priest tore his clothes. 'Why do we need any more witnesses?' he asked. **64** 'You have heard the blasphemy. What do you think?'

They all condemned him as worthy of death. **65** Then some began to spit at him; they blindfolded him, struck him with their fists, and said, 'Prophesy!' And the guards took him and beat him.

Peter disowns Jesus

66 While Peter was below in the courtyard, one of the servant-girls of the high priest came by. **67** When she saw Peter warming himself, she looked closely at him.

'You also were with that Nazarene, Jesus,' she said.

68 But he denied it. 'I don't know or understand what you're talking about,' he said, and went out into the entrance.*g*

69 When the servant-girl saw him there, she said again to those standing round them, 'This fellow is one of them.' **70** Again he denied it.

After a little while, those standing near said to Peter, 'Surely you are one of them, for you are a Galilean.'

---

g 68 Some early manuscripts *entrance and the cock crowed*

⁷¹ He began to call down curses, and he swore to them, 'I don't know this man you're talking about.'

⁷² Immediately the cock crowed the second time.ʰ Then Peter remembered the word Jesus had spoken to him: 'Before the cock crows twiceⁱ you will disown me three times.' And he broke down and wept.

Jesus before Pilate

15 Very early in the morning, the chief priests, with the elders, the teachers of the law and the whole Sanhedrin, made their plans. So they bound Jesus, led him away and handed him over to Pilate.

² 'Are you the king of the Jews?' asked Pilate.

'You have said so,' Jesus replied.

³ The chief priests accused him of many things. ⁴ So again Pilate asked him, 'Aren't you going to answer? See how many things they are accusing you of.'

⁵ But Jesus still made no reply, and Pilate was amazed.

⁶ Now it was the custom at the festival to release a prisoner whom the people requested. ⁷ A man called Barabbas was in prison with the rebels who had committed murder in the uprising. ⁸ The crowd came up and asked Pilate to do for them what he usually did.

⁹ 'Do you want me to release to you the king of the Jews?' asked Pilate, ¹⁰ knowing it was out of self-interest that the chief priests had handed Jesus over to him. ¹¹ But the chief

---

h 72 Some early manuscripts do not have *the second time*.
i 72 Some early manuscripts do not have *twice*.

priests stirred up the crowd to get Pilate to release Barabbas instead.

12 'What shall I do, then, with the one you call the king of the Jews?' Pilate asked them.

13 'Crucify him!' they shouted.

14 'Why? What crime has he committed?' asked Pilate.

But they shouted all the louder, 'Crucify him!'

15 Wanting to satisfy the crowd, Pilate released Barabbas to them. He had Jesus flogged, and handed him over to be crucified.

The soldiers mock Jesus

16 The soldiers led Jesus away into the palace (that is, the Praetorium) and called together the whole company of soldiers. 17 They put a purple robe on him, then twisted together a crown of thorns and set it on him. 18 And they began to call out to him, 'Hail, king of the Jews!' 19 Again and again they struck him on the head with a staff and spat on him. Falling on their knees, they paid homage to him. 20 And when they had mocked him, they took off the purple robe and put his own clothes on him. Then they led him out to crucify him.

The crucifixion of Jesus

21 A certain man from Cyrene, Simon, the father of Alexander and Rufus, was passing by on his way in from the country, and they forced him to carry the cross. 22 They brought Jesus to the place called Golgotha (which means 'the place of the skull'). 23 Then they offered him wine mixed with myrrh,

but he did not take it. ²⁴And they crucified him. Dividing up his clothes, they cast lots to see what each would get.

²⁵It was nine in the morning when they crucified him. ²⁶The written notice of the charge against him read: THE KING OF THE JEWS.

²⁷They crucified two rebels with him, one on his right and one on his left. [28]ᵃ ²⁹Those who passed by hurled insults at him, shaking their heads and saying, 'So! You who are going to destroy the temple and build it in three days, ³⁰come down from the cross and save yourself!' ³¹In the same way the chief priests and the teachers of the law mocked him among themselves. 'He saved others,' they said, 'but he can't save himself! ³²Let this Messiah, this king of Israel, come down now from the cross, that we may see and believe.' Those crucified with him also heaped insults on him.

The death of Jesus

³³At noon, darkness came over the whole land until three in the afternoon. ³⁴And at three in the afternoon Jesus cried out in a loud voice, '*Eloi, Eloi, lema sabachthani?*' (which means 'My God, my God, why have you forsaken me?').ᵇ

³⁵When some of those standing near heard this, they said, 'Listen, he's calling Elijah.'

³⁶Someone ran, filled a sponge with wine vinegar, put it on a staff, and offered it to Jesus to drink. 'Now leave him alone. Let's see if Elijah comes to take him down,' he said.

---

a 28 Some manuscripts include here words similar to Luke 22:37.
b 34 Psalm 22:1

37 With a loud cry, Jesus breathed his last.

38 The curtain of the temple was torn in two from top to bottom. 39 And when the centurion, who stood there in front of Jesus, saw how he died,c he said, 'Surely this man was the Son of God!'

40 Some women were watching from a distance. Among them were Mary Magdalene, Mary the mother of James the younger and of Joseph,d and Salome. 41 In Galilee these women had followed him and cared for his needs. Many other women who had come up with him to Jerusalem were also there.

The burial of Jesus

42 It was Preparation Day (that is, the day before the Sabbath). So as evening approached, 43 Joseph of Arimathea, a prominent member of the Council, who was himself waiting for the kingdom of God, went boldly to Pilate and asked for Jesus' body. 44 Pilate was surprised to hear that he was already dead. Summoning the centurion, he asked him if Jesus had already died. 45 When he learned from the centurion that it was so, he gave the body to Joseph. 46 So Joseph bought some linen cloth, took down the body, wrapped it in the linen, and placed it in a tomb cut out of rock. Then he rolled a stone against the entrance of the tomb. 47 Mary Magdalene and Mary the mother of Joseph saw where he was laid.

---

c 39 Some manuscripts *saw that he died with such a cry*
d 40 Greek *Joses*, a variant of *Joseph*; also in verse 47

Jesus has risen

16 When the Sabbath was over, Mary Magdalene, Mary the mother of James, and Salome bought spices so that they might go to anoint Jesus' body. ²Very early on the first day of the week, just after sunrise, they were on their way to the tomb ³and they asked each other, 'Who will roll the stone away from the entrance of the tomb?'

⁴But when they looked up, they saw that the stone, which was very large, had been rolled away. ⁵As they entered the tomb, they saw a young man dressed in a white robe sitting on the right side, and they were alarmed.

⁶'Don't be alarmed,' he said. 'You are looking for Jesus the Nazarene, who was crucified. He has risen! He is not here. See the place where they laid him. ⁷But go, tell his disciples and Peter, "He is going ahead of you into Galilee. There you will see him, just as he told you."'

⁸Trembling and bewildered, the women went out and fled from the tomb. They said nothing to anyone, because they were afraid.*

[The earliest manuscripts and some other ancient witnesses do not have verses 9 – 20.]

---

a 8 Some manuscripts have the following ending between verses 8 and 9, and one manuscript has it after verse 8 (omitting verses 9-20): *Then they quickly reported all these instructions to those around Peter. After this, Jesus himself also sent out through them from east to west the sacred and imperishable proclamation of eternal salvation. Amen.*

⁹When Jesus rose early on the first day of the week, he appeared first to Mary Magdalene, out of whom he had driven seven demons. ¹⁰She went and told those who had been with him and who were mourning and weeping. ¹¹When they heard that Jesus was alive and that she had seen him, they did not believe it.

¹²Afterwards Jesus appeared in a different form to two of them while they were walking in the country. ¹³These returned and reported it to the rest; but they did not believe them either.

¹⁴Later Jesus appeared to the Eleven as they were eating; he rebuked them for their lack of faith and their stubborn refusal to believe those who had seen him after he had risen.

¹⁵He said to them, 'Go into all the world and preach the gospel to all creation. ¹⁶Whoever believes and is baptised will be saved, but whoever does not believe will be condemned. ¹⁷And these signs will accompany those who believe: in my name they will drive out demons; they will speak in new tongues; ¹⁸they will pick up snakes with their hands; and when they drink deadly poison, it will not hurt them at all; they will place their hands on people who are ill, and they will get well.'

¹⁹After the Lord Jesus had spoken to them, he was taken up into heaven and he sat at the right hand of God. ²⁰Then the disciples went out and preached everywhere, and the Lord worked with them and confirmed his word by the signs that accompanied it.